THE
ADVENT
CALENDAR
RECIPE
BOOK

by

Karen Ette

Christmas recipes, fun-facts and reflections for Advent

Published November 2015.   Publisher: Scribblers Inc. Press
ISBN – 13:978-1519351517   ISBN – 10:1519351518

Contact the author via fancypanscafe@gmail.com

The Advent Calendar Recipe Book is packed with Christmas facts, poems and a festive recipe each day.

Do you know when the first Advent Calendar was made?

When is Stir-up Sunday?

Why does Easter move and Christmas doesn't?

Where was the largest snowman built?

How do you make an Impossible Pie?

What can you do if you have forgotten to buy a Christmas pudding?

Turkey leftovers? The perfect Turkey Curry.

Do you know how to play Donkey?

Why do we hang stockings up at Christmas?

Follow the nativity story each day during December and impress your guests with your Christmas knowledge and culinary skills.

HAPPY CHRISTMAS

Stir-up Sunday

The Sunday before the first in Advent is known as Stir-Up Sunday. This is because it embraces the British tradition of making the Christmas Pudding and was introduced, apparently, by Prince Albert, husband of Queen Victoria.

It was a time when families got together to make the pudding and where children learnt from their parents and grandparents what goes into the Christmas dessert. Most of us now tend to buy our Christmas puddings and will never experience the fun of stirring the pudding and popping in the odd coin which will be found on Christmas day, bringing health, wealth and happiness to the family for the coming year.

The term comes from the collect for the day in the Book of Common Prayer of 1549 and is used on the last Sunday before Advent in the Anglican Church:

Stir up, we beseech thee, O Lord, the wills of thy faithful people; that they, plenteously bringing forth the fruit of good works, may of thee be plenteously rewarded; through Jesus Christ our Lord. Amen.

Excita, quaesumus, Domine, tuorum fidelium voluntates: ut divini operis fructum propensius exsequentes, pietatis tuae remedia maiora percipiant: Per Christum Dominum nostrum. Amen.

It was thought that cooks, wives and servants would go to Church, hear the words 'stir up' and know that it was the day for making and stirring the Christmas puddings in plenty of time for Christmas Day.

A traditional Christmas pudding has thirteen ingredients to represent Jesus and his disciples. When family members take a turn in stirring, they should stir from east to west to remind them of the wise men who visited the child Jesus and brought him gifts. It is also customary to make a wish when it's your turn to stir.

Christmas Pudding

Here's a traditional recipe for a Christmas pudding for either 4 x1 pint puddings or 2 x 2 pint puddings.

Ingredients:
1   8oz (228g) golden caster sugar
2   8oz (228g) suet, or margarine
3   2lbs 4oz (567g) mixed dried fruit
4   8oz (228g) plain flour
5   2oz (57g) flaked almonds
6   Zest of 1 lemon
7   5 beaten eggs
8   A small cooking apple, peeled and chopped
9   1 level teaspoon ground cinnamon
10   1 level teaspoon mixed spice
11   1 level teaspoon nutmeg
12   Pinch of salt
13   5fl oz (28ml) brandy or rum

Mix together all the dry ingredients.

Stir in the eggs and brandy and mix together, with everyone taking a turn.

Put the mixture into 4x1pint pudding basins or 2x2 pint basins, which have been greased well.

Cut a circle of baking parchment for the top of each and wrap foil over the basins and tie securely with string - make a string handle from one side of the basin to the other so it's easier to pick the basin out of the pan after cooking.

Put the basins in to a large steamer or, if you don't have a steamer, use a large pan and put inverted saucers into it to stand the basins on.

Pour in boiling water, about a third of the way up the basins, then put the lid on and steam away. This will take about 5-6 hours and you will need to keep checking the water and replacing it so that the pan doesn't boil dry.

When cooked, store somewhere cool until you need them.

You will need to steam them again for another 2 hours before serving, or, you could cheat and pop them in the microwave for a few minutes.

1st December

Photograph by Syd Spence

Isaiah 9:2
The people walking in darkness
have seen a great light;
on those living in the land of deep darkness
a light has dawned.

Isaiah 9:6-7
For to us a child is born,
to us a son is given,
and the government will be on his shoulders.
And he will be called
Wonderful Counsellor, Mighty God,
Everlasting Father, Prince of Peace.

Advent Calendars probably date back to the1800s when families chalked lines on their door for every day in December up to Christmas Eve. There were also Advent clocks and a candle lit each day, known as Advent candles.

The tradition of printed Advent Calendars appears to have begun in Germany, when in 1902 a Christian Bookshop in Hamburg published an Advent Clock and in 1904 one was given away free in a newspaper called "Neues Tagblatt Stuttgart" (The Stuttgart Daily News).

The first paper Advent Calendars with windows were the brainchild of Gerhard Lang from Swabia in south-west Germany and their popularity spread until cardboard was rationed during World War 2 and calendars with pictures were not allowed. In 1946 the first Advent Calendar to be printed was by Richard Sellmer and Advent Calendars containing chocolate treats have been available since 1958.

Butternut Squash and Pear Soup

From this: To this:

You will need quite a large pan – one that holds about six or eight pints – for this gorgeous soup.

Ingredients:

1 large, or 2 smaller onions, peeled and chopped
2 tablespoons of butter or similar fat
1 pint stock – chicken or vegetable
1 lb (500g) butternut squash, peeled, seeded and chopped (or thereabouts)
2 pears, peeled, cored and chopped
1 teaspoon fresh thyme leaves
White pepper
Garam Masala
Cream or milk

This is what you do

Put about two tablespoons of butter into the pan and warm until melted. You can use margarine if you want, or if you are Vegan, then the oil of your choice, but olive oil doesn't work.

Add the chopped onion to the butter and leave to cook until tender.

When the onion is nice and soft, add a pint of stock (that's 20 fluid ozs or 2 cups) – chicken stock works best, but if you are vegetarian then it's best not to use this – maybe vegetable stock?

Then put in the squash, pear and thyme. Sprinkle in about ¼ teaspoon of white pepper and whack up the heat until it boils, then turn it down again, cover the pan and simmer until the squash is tender, this should take about 15 minutes.

When it's cooked, remove from the heat and liquidise.

Add about two teaspoons-full of garam masala, give it a good stir and taste. You can add more of the spice if you think it needs it. You can also add salt if you like more seasoning.

When it's nice and smooth, add about half-a-pint of double cream (or, if you prefer something a little less rich in cholesterol, you can use single cream or milk.) If you are vegan, you will need your oat milk here. You can make the soup as thick or runny as you so desire by adjusting the amount of cream or milk you put in.

So there you have it, scrummy, yummy Butternut Squash and pear soup.

2nd December

Luke 1:26-28
The Birth of Jesus Foretold
*In the sixth month of Elizabeth's pregnancy, God sent the angel Gabriel to Nazareth,
a town in Galilee, to a virgin pledged to be married to a man named Joseph, a
descendant of David. The virgin's name was Mary. The angel went to her and said,
"Greetings, you who are highly favoured! The Lord is with you."*

Christmas cakes are a delicious tradition that many make (or buy) and it may
be the only time of the year that fruitcake is eaten, especially one covered in
marzipan and Royal icing.

They started out as plum porridge. People of England fasted during the day
on Christmas Eve and ate plum porridge to line their stomachs before feasting
on Christmas Day. Then dried fruit spices and honey were added. The spices
were said to represent the eastern spices brought by the Magi. The mixture
was that of a Christmas pudding.

Thinking back to Stir-up-Sunday, families in the 1700s sometimes added flour,
butter and eggs to some of the Christmas pudding mixture and baked a cake
to keep for Easter. Later it became a cake for Christmas instead.

Cakes also used to be baked for Twelfth Night, the day that closed a period of
great celebration. These were covered in marzipan, or almond paste. In the
1640s the Puritans within the Government clamped down on celebration of
holy days, saints' days and Christmas, which remained in force until the
Restoration in 1660.

Christmas Day did remain a public holiday and some feasting was allowed, so
cakes were made and covered in marzipan

Oliver Cromwell didn't ban Christmas, but he did support the restrictions.

Traditional Christmas Cake

Before you begin, grease an 8 inch round or 7 inch square cake-tin and/or line with greaseproof paper. Tie a band of brown paper around the outside of the tin. Cut a double layer of greaseproof paper the same size as the bottom of the tin and cut a hole in the middle (fold it in four and snip a circle around the point about the size of a pound coin).

Ingredients:

2lbs (900g) of mixed, dried fruit
4 tablespoons brandy or rum (or orange juice)
8oz (228g) plain flour (or gluten-free flour)
half teaspoon salt
half teaspoon mixed spice (nutmeg is a nice addition too)
4 eggs (medium to large) - whisked
8oz (228g) soft brown sugar
8oz (228g) butter (unsalted if possible)
Grated rind of one lemon and one orange
2oz (57g) ground almonds
1 dessertspoon black treacle

This is what you do:

Put the fruit into a bowl and douse it with about four tablespoons of your favourite tipple - I prefer brandy, but rum is good too. Leave this to soak for an hour or two (overnight is better).

Put a tin of black treacle somewhere warm so that it becomes a bit runny for when you need it and pre-heat the oven to gas mark 1, 275F or 130 C.

Take your soaked fruit and add the grated rind of one lemon and one orange together with 2oz of ground almonds and stir it up and leave for a moment.

Sift the flour, salt and spices together.

In a **large** bowl, whisk the soft brown sugar with the softened butter until it's light and fluffy.

Add the whisked eggs to the sugar and butter, a little at a time (if it begins to look curdled, add some sifted flour). Eggs all in, fold in the flour and spices.

Add a dessertspoon of the (now runny) black treacle and stir it in followed closely by the fruit mixture. When it's thoroughly mixed, spoon it into your prepared tin. Cover the top with the greaseproof with the hole in and place on a low shelf in the oven. If you have a fan oven, you will need to place a teaspoon on the greaseproof paper to prevent it from blowing away.

It will take about four-and-a- quarter to four-and-three-quarter hours to cook. You can leave it in the oven for an hour afterwards.

3rd December

Photograph by Syd Spence

Luke 1:29-32

God sent the angel Gabriel to Nazareth, a town in Galilee, to a virgin pledged to be married to a man named Joseph, a descendant of David. The virgin's name was Mary. The angel went to her and said, "Greetings, you who are highly favoured! The Lord is with you."Mary was greatly troubled at his words and wondered what kind of greeting this might be. But the angel said to her, "Do not be afraid, Mary; you have found favour with God. You will conceive and give birth to a son, and you are to call him Jesus. He will be great and will be called the Son of the Most High.

The Angel Gabriel

Gabriel mans "man of God" or "strength of God".

Gabriel stands in the presence of God and this is how he describes himself to Zachariah earlier in Luke, chapter 1 (verse 19): "I am Gabriel. I stand in the presence of God and have been sent to speak to you and to tell you the good news."

Unfortunately, Gabriel tends to frighten people and has to tell them: "do not be afraid."

Only two angels are named in the Protestant Bible: Gabriel and Michael.

Gabriel is mentioned in both the Old Testament in Daniel when he is told to explain a vision to the prophet, and the New when he tells Zachariah that his son (John the Baptist) will pave the way for the Messiah (Jesus) and, more famously, he tells Mary that her son will be called Jesus.

Pickled Red Cabbage

This is a quick, simple and easy recipe for pickled red cabbage, although it does take two days.

Ingredients:

1 Red Cabbage
Salt – a couple of tablespoons
Malt vinegar (spiced is nice)
Some sterilised jars

One decent sized cabbage makes quite a few jars. All you need to do is slice it up, as fine or as chunky as you like it, and put a layer into a large bowl, sprinkle on salt, then add another layer, more salt, and so on until all the cabbage is in the bowl. Cover and leave overnight.

Next day, Rinse the excess salt off using a colander and pack the shredded/sliced cabbage into jars. Pour vinegar into each jar until it covers the cabbage, and seal. You can use ordinary malt vinegar or the pickling/spiced variety - your choice.

As you do this you will see a fascinating transformation; the blue-ish cabbage (alkaline) will turn bright red as you pour over the vinegar (acid). So that's the school connection - good old litmus paper testing.

It is best to leave the pickled cabbage for about three weeks so at Christmas you will be eating it at its best. It is great with cold turkey or cold roast ham.

4th December

Photograph by Rachael Mott

Luke 1:34-37

From: **The Message**

Mary said to the angel, "But how? I've never slept with a man."
The angel answered:
The Holy Spirit will come upon you,
the power of the Highest hover over you;
Therefore, the child you bring to birth
will be called Holy, Son of God.
"And did you know that your cousin Elizabeth conceived a son, old as she is?
Everyone called her barren, and here she is six months pregnant!
Nothing, you see, is impossible with God."

My Grandma made the best puddings in the world – I loved seeing her make them, and they were always there after our dinner. On special occasions, such as Christmas Nativity plays and Harvest Festivals, Gran would make an Impossible Pie, which any magician would have been proud of. I loved these occasions when maiden aunts would visit and always gave me a bar of chocolate or some loose change from their pig-skin purses – not quite the silk purse, but very soft leather nevertheless.

Gran would just throw a pile of ingredients into a dish and stir them really well. Then she would wave her 'special' wooden spoon over it and say "stir it clockwise as far as possible, stir it anti-clockwise as far as possible and make me a pie – IMPOSSIBLE!" – the magic worked in the oven and we had a pie with custard every time.

Impossible Pie

For a family-sized pie you will need to butter a ten-inch pie dish (that's twenty-five centimetres if you don't do Imperial measurements).

Then, into a large bowl put:

4 beaten eggs

1 oz (28g) soft margarine (or butter)

6 oz (170g) white sugar

2 oz (57g) plain flour (use gluten free or rice flour if you need to)

½ teaspoon baking powder

2 cups of milk

Pinch of salt (about ¼ teaspoon)

1 teaspoon of vanilla essence

3 oz (85g) desiccated coconut

Mix everything together really well and pour into the pie dish.

Bake the pie in a warm to moderate oven at Gas 3-4 (that's 160-180C or 325 – 350F) for an hour.

You'll be amazed when you take the pie from the oven, as you will have a crust on the base, custard in the middle and a coconut topping.

5th December

Photograph by Syd Spence

Luke 1:39-45
Mary Visits Elizabeth
Soon afterwards Mary got ready and hurried off to a town in the hill country of Judea. She went into Zechariah's house and greeted Elizabeth. When Elizabeth heard Mary's greeting, the baby moved within her. Elizabeth was filled with the Holy Spirit and said in a loud voice, "You are the most blessed of all women, and blessed is the child you will bear! Why should this great thing happen to me, that my Lord's mother comes to visit me? For as soon as I heard your greeting, the baby within me jumped with gladness. How happy you are to believe that the Lord's message to you will come true!"

Christmas Tree Decorations

During the 17th Century Christmas markets sold both tress and decorations. To begin with, the decorations were red or white, symbolising knowledge and innocence. Some records tell that coloured paper flowers were also sold plus candles, candy-twists, wax figures and gingerbread*.

Then came tinsel, made from **real** silver and during Victorian times Christmas trees were decorated with tinsel, beads, ornaments made from silver wire and candles. Gifts were also hung from the branches of larger trees. Glass baubles became available in in 1882 the first electric lights were patented.

Now would be a good time to make some **Christmas Tree Biscuits**

Ingredients:
7oz (200g) plain flour
½ teaspoon bicarbonate of soda
½ teaspoon cinnamon
½ teaspoon ground ginger
4oz (100g) butter or margarine
2oz (50g) caster sugar
4 cardamom seeds
2 tablespoons ground almonds
3oz (75g) black treacle
1 beaten egg yolk

For the Icing:
3oz (75g) sieved icing sugar
About 1 tablespoon warm water (+ food colouring)

Before you begin you might want to switch the oven on – it needs to be fairly hot at gas mark 5, 190C and 375F.
Put your tin of black treacle somewhere warm to make it more runny.
Take a large bowl and sieve in the flour, bicarbonate of soda, cinnamon and ground ginger.
Spoon the (now runny) black treacle into a saucepan with the butter, or margarine and melt them together gently.
Take the 4 cardamom seeds, split them open and crush the kernels, then add them to the melted mixture. To this, add the caster sugar and ground almonds.
Combine the melted ingredients with the dry and add one beaten egg yolk
Work it all together to form a smooth dough, wrap it in cling film and leave in the fridge for about 20-30 minutes.
Half an hour later, lightly flour a surface and your rolling pin, and roll out the dough (after you have taken off the cling-film) to about a quarter of an inch thick (that's about 5mm).
Use cutters to make the desired shapes, or do it free hand: hearts, stars, etc.
Place them on a greased baking sheet (or one lined with grease-proof paper) and bake for about 10-12 minutes until they are just firm to the touch. As soon as you remove them from the oven, make a hole in each, with a suitable implement, for the ribbon to be threaded through. Put them onto wire trays to cool where they will 'firm up' nicely.
When they are cold, you can decorate them using either bought coloured icing, or make your own by adding colouring to sieved icing sugar and putting it into a piping bag. You can stick on silver balls (edible ones), sugar flowers, etc. – Go on, be creative. Lastly, thread a ribbon through and tie to form a loop, and then you're all ready to hang on the tree (not you, the decorations).

Of course, you don't have to hang them on the tree to gather dust, and then throw to the birds after twelfth night, you can actually eat them.

6th December

Photograph by Syd Spence

Luke 1:46-56

Mary's Song

And Mary said:
"My soul glorifies the Lord
and my spirit rejoices in God my Saviour,
for he has been mindful
of the humble state of his servant.
From now on all generations will call me blessed,
for the Mighty One has done great things for me—
holy is his name.
His mercy extends to those who fear him,
from generation to generation.
He has performed mighty deeds with his arm;
he has scattered those who are proud in their inmost thoughts.
He has brought down rulers from their thrones
but has lifted up the humble.
He has filled the hungry with good things
but has sent the rich away empty.
He has helped his servant Israel,
remembering to be merciful
to Abraham and his descendants forever,
just as he promised our ancestors."
Mary stayed with Elizabeth for about three months and then returned home.

Butterfly Cakes or Angel Cakes

To make Angel/Butterfly/Fairy cakes you will need:

12 paper cake cases put into a patty tin

Set the oven to warm at gas 4-5, 350-375F, 180-190C.

Into a large bowl put:
6 oz (170g) softened butter or margerine (Olive spread is brilliant in sponge cakes)
6 oz (170g) of caster sugar
6 oz (170g) of self-raising flour
3 beaten eggs

Mix everything together really well. You could add a few drops of vanilla essence too.

Don't be tempted to add baking powder thinking it will give you extra lift - it will when they first rise, but then they'll flop, and you don't want that to happen.

Put a spoonful of the mix into each cake case and pop into the oven for about 15-20 minutes.

Whilst they are cooking, mix together
4oz (115g) of sifted icing sugar
2 oz (55g) butter - beat well to make your butter-cream.

When the cakes are done, leave them to cool, then slice the tops off and cut them in half.
Ice each cake with the butter-cream and press the tops (wings) into it.
Dust with sifted icing sugar and you have angel cakes.

If you would like chocolate cakes, substitute 1 oz (25g) flour with same amount of cocoa. Add cocoa to the butter-cream if you would like that to be chocolate too. If you plump for the pink, yellow and white cakes, just separate the mix into 3 small bowls and add a drop of cake colouring.

7th December

Photograph by Syd Spence

Matthew 1:19-21

Because Joseph, Mary's husband was faithful to the law, and yet did not want to expose her to public disgrace, he had in mind to divorce her quietly.
But after he had considered this, an angel of the Lord appeared to him in a dream and said, "Joseph son of David, do not be afraid to take Mary home as your wife, because what is conceived in her is from the Holy Spirit. She will give birth to a son, and you are to give him the name Jesus, because he will save his people from their sins."

Why is Christmas always on the same date and yet Easter moves?

Each year the question arises as to why Easter moves when Christmas is always on the same date - 25th December. Christmas never changes and is set with Advent paving the way to a celebration of the Messiah's birth.

Candlemas is another Christian celebration that takes place on the same day - 2nd February. This is the last festival in the Christian year that is dated by reference to Christmas and those which follow are with reference to Easter.

Easter is a moveable feast – and when you know how, it's easy to find out when Easter Day will be each year.

Going back to Candlemas, (mid-winter) this is day between the winter solstice in December and the spring (vernal) equinox in March, which is why it is always the same. Equinox means equal; when the hours between sunrise and sunset are equal. The spring equinox is one of 20th-21st-22nd March.

The next marker is the full moon after the equinox.

If you know when the full moon after the vernal equinox is, the Sunday after that will be Easter Sunday. So that is why Easter moves. The earliest Easter can be is 22nd March and the latest, 25th April.

Hot Cross Bun and Butter Pudding

This is a variation on Bread and Butter Pudding and can also be made with teacakes instead of hot-cross buns.

Butter a 2-pint baking dish and set the oven to Gas 4, 350F or 180C (less for a fan assisted oven).

Ingredients:

8 hot-cross buns or teacakes
½ pint of milk (whole milk is best, but semi-skimmed is fine too)
2 tablespoons of double cream
2 oz (55g) sugar (Demerara, caster or granulated)
3 eggs
Nutmeg (grated)

This is what you do:

Slice the buns in half, butter them, and then slice them in half again. Layer them into the buttered baking dish.

Put the eggs into a bowl and whisk them, then add the milk, cream and sugar and give them another good whisk. Pour over the buttered buns and grate a little nutmeg over the surface.

Bake for about 35-40 minutes.

It's nice hot, but can be served cold too – and if you really want to, you can add more custard.

8th December

Matthew 1:22-25

All this took place to fulfil what the Lord had said through the prophet: 'The virgin will conceive and give birth to a son, and they will call him Immanuel'
(which means 'God with us').
When Joseph woke up, he did what the angel of the Lord had commanded him and took Mary home as his wife. But he did not consummate their marriage until she gave birth to a son. And he gave him the name Jesus.

Christmas Trees

The earliest record of decorated trees appearing at Christmas was in Alsace around 1520, and in the early 1600s the tradition of bringing a fir tree indoors at Christmas and putting pretty objects on it was well-established in Germany. A little later, candles adorned the branches.

In 1789, Queen Charlotte, wife of George III, is said to have placed a decorated tree in Windsor Castle.

Prince Albert was always thought to have introduced the custom of bringing decorated fir trees into the home in Britain.

Once Queen Victoria had adopted the tradition, there was no stopping the Victorians from doing what they did best, and decorated trees graced their households.

If you would like something nice to nibble on whilst you decorate your tree, you could try some homemade spiced nuts.

Nuts

Put the oven on to warm up to gas 4, 350F or 180C.

You will need:

A lightly oiled baking sheet

2 oz (50-60g) shelled nuts (walnuts, blanched almonds, hazelnuts, cashews, macadamia, peanuts, etc.)
4 oz (100g) caster sugar
1 teaspoon of cinnamon
½ teaspoon of ground ginger
A little grated nutmeg
½ a teaspoon of coriander
Chilli powder or paprika – optional
1 egg

In a bowl mix the caster sugar, cinnamon, ground ginger, grated nutmeg and coriander. You can add chilli or paprika if you would like to liven them up a little.

Separate the egg.

You can use the yolk in the Christmas-tree biscuits, as you only need the white for this recipe. Or, if you have already made the tree biscuits, you'll have a redundant egg yolk waiting to be used.

Beat the egg white until it's thick, but not like meringue.

Dip each nut into the egg white and then the sugar and spice mix, making sure they are well coated, and place them on the baking sheet/tray. Don't worry if there's some spice mix left, you'll need it later.

Put the tray into the oven and bake for about 15-20 minutes. Take them out of the oven and sprinkle with the remaining sugar and spice mix, then put them back in for another 5 minutes.

Allow them to cool and there you have it. Nuts to nibble at Christmas.

9th December

Micah 5:2-5
The Coming Messiah
"But you, Bethlehem Ephrathah,
Though you are little among the thousands of Judah,
Yet out of you shall come forth to Me
The One to be Ruler in Israel,
Whose goings forth are from of old,
From everlasting."
Therefore He shall give them up,
Until the time that she who is in labour has given birth;
Then the remnant of His brethren
Shall return to the children of Israel.
And He shall stand and feed His flock
In the strength of the LORD,
In the majesty of the name of the LORD *His God;*
And they shall abide,
For now He shall be great
To the ends of the earth;
And this One shall be peace.

Christingle

The tradition of **Christingle** originated in Germany

One Christmas Eve, Bishop Johannes de bottom de Watteville decided to make a simple symbol to give to the children in the Moravian Church to explain the love of Jesus and the true meaning of Christmas. He gave each child a lit candle wrapped in red ribbon with a prayer, which said:

"Lord Jesus, kindle a flame in these dear children's hearts".

In 1968, John Pensom of *The Children's Society* introduced Christingle services to the Anglican Church from where it spread.

A Christingle is symbolic and made up of:

An orange which represents the world

A red ribbon tied around it representing the blood of Christ

Dried fruits or sweets skewered on four cocktail sticks pushed into the orange, representing the fruits of the earth and the four seasons

A white candle pushed into the centre of the orange, representing Jesus Christ as the light of the world.

10th December

Photograph by Syd Spence

Luke 2:1-5
The birth of Jesus

In those days Caesar Augustus issued a decree that a census should be taken of the entire Roman world. (This was the first census that took place while Quirinius was governor of Syria.) And everyone went to their own town to register.
So Joseph also went up from the town of Nazareth in Galilee to Judea, to Bethlehem the town of David, because he belonged to the house and line of David. He went there to register with Mary, who was pledged to be married to him and was expecting a child.

The Game of Donkey

You will need one pack of playing cards, plus a joker.

The dealer deals **all** of the cards to the players.

Players look at their cards and put down any pairs they have, face up, for example, two red Queens (Queen of Hearts and Queen of Diamonds) or two black threes (three of Spades and three of Clubs).

The dealer starts and offers his hand, face down, to the player on their left.

That player takes a card and adds it to their hand.

This player then sees if the selected card makes a pair with their original cards. If so, the pair is discarded, face up. The player who just took a card then offers their hand, face down, to the person to their left and so on.

Players are allowed to shuffle their hand before offering it to the player on their left.

The objective of the game is to continue to take cards, putting down the pairs until all players except one have no cards.

The player left with the Joker is the Donkey.

Chocolate Haystacks

This is a quick, easy, recipe.

You will need a large bowl and twenty-four cake cases. You can rest these in patty tins, but you don't need to.

Put 10 oz (285g) slightly crushed (only slightly) cornflakes into your bowl

Add 14 oz (400g) dried milk POWDER (not granules) and

2-3 oz (about 70g) of cocoa powder and mix together well.

In a saucepan melt

14 oz (400g) block margarine with
16 oz [1 lb] (450g) golden syrup

Pour this into the cornflake mixture and stir it all together - the easiest and best way is to use your hands (then you have a good excuse for licking your fingers).

Put a good spoonful of the mix into each of the cake cases and leave them somewhere cool to set.

To turn these into a 'proper' dessert, serve with fresh strawberries or raspberries and clotted cream.

11th December

Photograph by Syd Spence

Isaiah 7:14
Therefore the Lord himself will give you a sign: the virgin will conceive and give birth to a son, and will call him Immanuel.

Mincemeat

The word mince in mincemeat comes from Middle English - *mincen,* and Old French – *mincier.* These both trace back to Latin - *minutia* meaning **smallness**.

The word mincemeat is from minced meat, in other words, finely chopped meat.

Recipes for a pie filling from 15th, 16th, and 17th century England describe it as a mixture of meat and fruit. These early recipes also included wine and sometimes vinegar.

Then in the 18th century, distilled spirits, most often Brandy, were used instead.

Spices like cloves, mace and nutmeg were used common in late medieval and renaissance meat dishes.

Sugar was added which made mincemeat less savoury and developed its use for desserts.

Homemade Mincemeat

You can't beat homemade mincemeat, however it can be difficult to keep as the juice from the apples can start to ferment, but if you melt the suet first, this coats the fruit and stops that happening. This recipe makes three, 1 lb jars.

Ingredients:
4 oz (110g) cooking apples, cored and chopped very finely - you can leave the skin on if you want, or take it off if you prefer.
2 oz (55g) shredded suet (or grated hard margarine instead)
2 oz (55g) sultanas
2 oz (55g) currants
3 oz (85g) raisins
2 oz (55g) mixed, candied peel
2 oz (55g) chopped glace cherries
3 oz (85g) soft brown sugar
The grated zest and juice of a lemon and an orange
1 oz (25g) flaked almonds – this is optional
1 teaspoon ground, mixed spice, plus a little (¼ teaspoon) cinnamon
A little freshly ground nutmeg adds that extra oooh factor, but not essential.

Put everything into a large oven-proof mixing bowl and stir. Cover the bowl with a tea towel and leave the mix to stand overnight so that the fruit can absorb the spices.

You will need to sterilise your jam jars and lids – a hot cycle in a dishwasher does this, or you can wash them in hot, soapy water, rinse them in hot water and put them into the oven at 375F, 190C, gas 5 for about 5-10 minutes. Take care when you remove them to cool.

Next day, switch the oven on to a low heat: 225F, 120C, gas ¼.
Stir the mixture and cover the bowl with foil. Put the bowl into the oven for 2½ - 3 hours. When you take it out, the mincemeat will look very runny and fatty. Leave it to cool and stir occasionally until the fat has set around the fruit. If you would like boozy mincemeat, add a couple of tablespoons of your favourite tipple – whisky, rum, brandy, sherry.

Put your homemade mincemeat into your sterile jars, cover and seal.

12th December

Luke 2:6-7
So it was, that while they were there, the days were completed for her to be delivered. And she brought forth her firstborn Son, and wrapped Him in swaddling cloths, and laid Him in a manger, because there was no room for them in the inn.

Snowmen

The earliest recorded sighting of a snowman was depicted in a work called the Book of Hours which dates back to 1367 - it was a sketched illustration.

Picture: Wikimedia Commons

A town called Bethel in Maine, USA, holds the record for the largest snowmen. In 2008 one stood 122ft and 1in tall (37.21m) and was called 'Olympia Snowe' after their Senator.

In 1999 another snowman called 'Angus, King of the Mountain' after the then governor of Maine, stood 113ft 7 inches tall (34.62 m)

Peppermint Snowmen

These little chaps can be served at the end of a meal instead of the usual after-dinner mints.

Ingredients:

1 small (218g) tin of sweetened, **condensed** milk
1 lb 2 oz (500g) sifted icing sugar
A few drops of peppermint essence
A few drops of red food colouring
Edible silver balls
Liquorice laces and perhaps Jelly Tots or Dolly Mixtures for decoration.

This is what you do:

Sieve the icing sugar into a large bowl.

Add the condensed milk and peppermint essence. If you are making them with and for, children, they may not like peppermint, but you can always leave that out.

Mix everything together well until you have a firm, doughy ball.

You can make coloured scarves for the snowmen by taking a small piece of the dough and adding food colouring and working it really well.

With the rest of the dough, make about thirty small balls – you could make fifteen slightly larger than the other fifteen so you have different sized bodies to heads.

Put the heads on top of the bodies

Make scarves from the coloured dough. You can then decorate using silver balls for eyes, buttons, etc. Put them on one side to 'dry'.

Enjoy your minty snowmen.

13th December

Photograph by Syd Spence

Isaiah 11:1-2
The branch from Jesse

A shoot will come up from the stump of Jesse;
from his roots a Branch will bear fruit.
The Spirit of the LORD will rest on him –
the Spirit of wisdom and of understanding,
the Spirit of counsel and of might,
the Spirit of the knowledge

Mince Pies

Tradition says that if you eat a mince pie in someone else's house it means you'll have a 'happy month'.

The first mince pies were called *mutton pyes, shrid pyes* and, believe it or not, *Christmas pyes*. The filling back in the 13th/14th centuries was minced meat with suet, which had fruits added and spices such as nutmeg, cloves, cinnamon, etc. These spices were thought to be representative of the gifts of the Magi.

During the English Civil War (1642–1651) the Puritans (English Protestants) said that the 'savoury pie' was associated with Catholic 'idolatry', supposedly, and they didn't approve. The pies won through and the tradition of eating them at Christmas carried on until Victorian times, but they had become sweeter and changed in shape. They were originally larger and oblong (sometimes called a 'coffin') but became smaller and more in the shape of a crib.

Having made your mincemeat, it's time for **Mince Pies**

You will need a 3-inch (7.5 cm) pastry cutter for the bases and a 2½-inch (6 cm) one for the lids (or you can cut stars like the ones below), plus a greased patty tin which holds 12, and, of course, a rolling pin.
Pre-heat your oven to 400F, 200C, gas 6.

Ingredients for 24 mince pies:
7 oz (200g) of **plain** flour
1 oz (25g) of icing sugar
Pinch of salt.
2 oz (55g) of butter at room temperature
2 oz (55g) of lard
3-4 tablespoons **cold** water

This is what you do:
Sieve the flour, icing sugar and salt into a bowl to get as much air into it as possible.
Add the fat. Butter and lard to give a lovely crisp texture, but you can use hard margarine and/or white fat instead, but you will lose out on flavour.
Rub in the fat until it resembles breadcrumbs.
Add 3-4 tablespoons of **cold** water and bring the mix together to form a smooth, doughy ball (you may need to add a little more water, but take care not to add too much as the pastry will be tough).
Wrap the pastry in cling-film (or put into a polythene bag) and leave to rest in the fridge for 20-30 minutes. Don't skimp on this. Whilst it rests, the gluten in the flour will react with the water and the pastry will be more elastic and easier to roll out, and it won't shrink when you bake it.
Flour your work-surface and rolling pin and take the pastry from the fridge and remove the cling-film. Divide it into two and roll out one half to about ⅛ inch (3mm) thick. Cut the bases with the larger cutter, and put them into the patty tin. Put a teaspoon of your homemade mincemeat into each one and cut the same number of lids using the smaller cutter. Place the lids on top of the mincemeat. You can wet the edges first to help them to seal. Make a small cut (½ cm) in the centre of each lid (unless you have made stars then there is no need). You can brush the pies with beaten egg or milk, and pop them into the warm oven for 20-30 minutes until they are a light golden colour.
Sprinkle them with caster sugar and you should do this as soon as they come out of the oven, or if you prefer icing sugar, leave them to cool before dusting them with it.

Twelve mince pies = 12 happy months.

14th December

Photograph Syd Spence

Luke 2:8-9
And there were shepherds living out in the fields near by, keeping watch over their flocks at night. An angel of the Lord appeared to them, and the glory of the Lord shone around them, and they were terrified.

The shepherds play a significant role in the birth narrative of Luke.

Near Bethlehem was a place called Migdal Eder, meaning the Tower of the Flock. The shepherds on this particular hill looked after temple sheep, the first-born male lambs that were bred for sacrifice in the temple.

Generation after generation of shepherds looked after the sacred sheep and these were poor, lowly people who often risked their lives to bring back an animal that had strayed.

When an angel appeared and told them of the birth of 'the lamb of God' they were terrified, understandably, but the significance is that the saviour born that day would be the one to pay the ultimate sin-sacrifice.

Mutton Pies

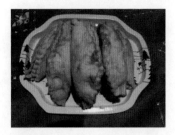

The pies are not usually filled with mutton as this needs long, slow cooking first, but does give an extremely good flavour.

The quickest and easiest way to make the pies is to use:
1lb (500g) lamb mince
1 finely chopped large onion
1 tablespoon lard, dripping or vegetable oil for cooking.
1/2 pint thick gravy

Gently cook the onion in the fat/oil. Don't let it brown though. When it is soft, drain off the excess fat and add the mince. Let it cook slowly for about ten minutes.
Stir in some of gravy, but not so that it is runny. Season.
You can add chilli if you would like a little extra warmth, or paprika for a gentler touch.

For the pastry use half fat to flour:
1 lb (500g) **plain** flour
8 oz (250g) lard
Salt
1/4 teaspoon mustard powder
5-6 tablespoons of cold water

Rub the lard into the flour until it resembles breadcrumbs and add a good sprinkling of salt and mustard powder. Add the cold water until the pastry comes together without being sticky.
Wrap in cling-film and let it rest in the fridge for 20 minutes to half-an-hour. As with the mince pies on day 13, don't skimp on this because whilst it rests, the gluten in the flour will react with the water and the pastry will be more elastic and easier to roll out – and it won't shrink when you bake it.
Warm the oven to 400F, 200C, gas 6
When the pastry is well chilled take off its cling-film coat and cut in half (it's easier to work in smaller amounts). Roll out one half on a floured surface to about ¼ inch thick and use a saucer to cut out circles of the pastry. Put a spoonful of the mince in the centre of each pastry circle, wet round the edge of the circle with cold water and pull the sides up and over the mince and squeeze it together to seal. Put the pies onto a greased baking sheet and pop into the oven for about 20-25 minutes. Do the same with the remaining pastry.

15th December

Photograph by Syd Spence

Luke 2:10-11

Then the angel said to them, "Do not be afraid, for behold, I bring you good tidings of great joy which will be to all people. [11] For there is born to you this day in the city of David a Saviour, who is Christ the Lord."

Stilton Cheese

A few Stilton facts are:

It can only be produced in the three Counties - Derbyshire, Nottinghamshire and Leicestershire.

It must be made from locally produced milk that has been pasteurised before use.

It can only be made in a cylindrical shape.

It must be allowed to form its own coat or crust.

It must never be pressed.

It must have the magical blue veins radiating from the centre of the cheese.

It even has its own website!

So, if you would like to to find out more about Stilton try:

http://www.stiltoncheese.co.uk

Stilton and Broccoli Soup

Stilton is traditionally given and eaten at Christmas, and as the amount bought can sometimes be misjudged, there is often some left over to make this delicious soup.

Ingredients:

1 chopped onion
2 stalks of celery – de-stringed and chopped
1 large or 2 small leeks – finely chopped.
2 oz (56g) butter
Approx. 1 pint (570 ml) vegetable or chickien stock.
2 heads of broccoli
1 tbsp mixed herbs
White pepper
4 oz (110g) – or thereabouts – Stilton cheese
Milk or cream.
And if you have some left-over Brussels sprouts, you could always put them in too.

Here's what you do:

Melt the butter in a large saucepan and add the chopped onion, celery and leeks.

Sweat them over a low heat until they are soft - but definitely don't let them brown.

Add the broccoli – you can include some stalks if they are not too thick and woody, mixed herbs and white pepper.

Make enough stock to just cover the broccoli and simmer until everything is cooked and all the ingredients are soft.

Liquidise with either a hand blender or in a liquidiser/food processor.

Crumble the Stilton into the hot liquid and stir thoroughly. Keep stirring until the cheese has melted.

Taste and adjust seasoning.

Stilton is salty so you may not need to add any. If the soup is too thick for your liking, add milk (or cream) until you reach the correct consistency.

16th December

Luke 2:12
And this will be the sign to you: You will find a Babe wrapped in swaddling cloths,
lying in a manger.

Away in a Manger

Away in a manger, No crib for His bed
The little Lord Jesus, Laid down His sweet head
The stars in the bright sky, Looked down where He lay
The little Lord Jesus, Asleep on the hay

Away in a Manger is one of the most popular and most often sung Christmas carols of the English-speaking world.

It is thought that the first two verses were first published in 1885 in a book called *The Little Children's Book for Schools and Families,* in Philadelphia, USA, with the third verse which first appearing in a Charles H. Gabriel collection from 1892.

The author of *Away in a Manger* is not known and it is thought to have originally been a poem and the words have been set to a number of different tunes. It has been suggested, without proof that it may have been written by Martin Luther.

The words are not based on the actual text of the Bible and the Bible does not make any references to cattle at the birth, nor does it say that Jesus did not cry as a baby.

Lemon Fridge Cake

This is a 'make it the day before' recipe.

Line a 1lb loaf tin with cling-film (leave plenty of over-hang to cover).

Top tip: Pop the lemons into the microwave for about thirty seconds to make them more juicy.

Ingredients:

4 fresh eggs – separated
4oz (113g) butter (unsalted is best) at room temperature
1 packet of sponge fingers or trifle sponges
Zest and juice of 2 lemons (un-waxed if possible)
½ pint (284ml) double or whipping cream
Chocolate flakes

This is what you do:

Separate the eggs and put the whites to one side (you can make meringues later). Whisk the yolks.

Put the butter into a bowl with the caster sugar and cream them together.

Add the beaten egg yolks, lemon juice and zest and beat the mix really well until it's fluffy and very pale.

Place a layer of the sponges into the base of the loaf tin. Spoon on half the mixture until the sponge is covered then add another layer of sponge, top with the rest of the mixture and put a final layer of sponge on the top of that.

Pull the cling film over the top to seal it in all snugly and pop into the fridge overnight.

You may now lick your fingers.

Before you serve this gorgeous lemony, sweet, heavenly dessert, you will need to whisk up about half a pint (284ml) of cream – whipping or double.

Turn the cake out onto a serving plate, pull off the cling-film and cover with the whipped cream. Sprinkle the top with chocolate (break up a flake) or you can use strips of lemon zest or some toasted nuts.

17th December

Photograph by Rob Newton

Luke 2:13-14
And suddenly there was with the angel a multitude of the heavenly host praising God
and saying:
"Glory to God in the highest,
And on earth peace, goodwill toward men!"

When the Angels appeared to shepherds on a lonely hillside they were scared, terrified. Gabriel had told Mary 'Fear not' and said the same to Joseph. The same words were said to the shepherds: 'Fear not'.

Angels are supernatural, not of this world. Imagine how the shepherds would have felt; they were going about their business, some probably falling asleep when an Angel appears, and if that wasn't frightening enough, a whole crowd join him. In Luke 2 verse 13 it says: 'Suddenly!' – there were no angels one minute and the next a 'multitude'.

If the shepherds saw the angels, then surely they must have also been visible in the town of Bethlehem?

We shall never know.

Another popular legend about Angels is that of the Angels of Mons who are reputed to have protected soldiers in the British Army at the Battle of Mons on the 23rd August 1914, at the beginning of World War 1.

Glorious Cheesecake

Ideally, you'll need a round, 8 inch (that's 21½cms or 215 mm) loose-bottomed cake tin that you should lightly grease.

Ingredients:
Base:
4 oz (115g) Digestive biscuits
4 oz (115g) Gingernut biscuits
4 oz (115g) butter
1 tablespoon golden syrup
Filling:
10 -12 fl oz double cream (about ½ pint, 284ml)
4 oz (115g) cream cheese
Juice of ½ a lemon
5 oz (140g) sieved icing sugar

This is what you do:

Crush the biscuits together: you can put them into a plastic bag and give them a good bashing with a rolling pin (very therapeutic) or whizz them in a food-processor.

Melt the butter in a saucepan with a tablespoon of golden syrup. When these are nicely runny, pour in the crushed biscuits and stir thoroughly. Put the biscuit mix into the cake tin and press it down into place. Pop into the fridge and leave whilst you make the filling.

Pour the double cream into a bowl and whip it until really thick. Put this to one side.

In another, large bowl, put the cream cheese, squeeze in the lemon juice and mix them together.

Sieve the icing sugar into the cheese mix. Stir thoroughly and then add the whipped cream and stir that in too. (You can add flavouring to the mix, for example, Baileys Cream, Tia Maria.)

Take the cake-tin from the fridge and put the mixture on top of the biscuit base. Leave in the fridge to chill for a couple of hours.

When you remove the cheesecake from the fridge and put it onto a serving plate, you can add a topping of your choice: chocolate, fresh strawberries, cherries in Kirsch, there's so much choice for enjoying the indulgence of this cheesecake.

18th December

Luke 2:15-16

So it was, when the angels had gone away from them into heaven, that the shepherds said to one another, "Let us now go to Bethlehem and see this thing that has come to pass, which the Lord has made known to us." And they came with haste and found Mary and Joseph, and the Babe lying in a manger.

A manger scene, or nativity are present in many places during Advent and have figures representing the baby Jesus, Mary and Joseph, shepherds and often the wise men. Animals such as lambs, donkeys and an ox are typical members of a nativity scene too.

It is believed that St Francis of Assisi created the very first manger scene way back in 1223 after he had visited the Holy Land and seen where Jesus was born. He wanted to place Christ at the heart of Christmas rather than materialism and gift giving.

St Francis's nativity had real people and animals and was staged in a cave. Pope Honorius III blessed the nativity.

By the end of the 19th century nativity scenes became popular beyond Catholic settings and different nativity scenes emerged in different countries.

A tradition in England was that of baking a mince pie in the shape of a crib to hold the baby Jesus until mealtime when the pie was eaten. In the 17th century, when Christmas celebrations were banned by the Puritans, they also passed a law to prohibit such pies, calling them "Idolatry in crust".

Cheese straws (and cheese biscuits)

Manger in French it means, 'to eat' and when thinking about manger, you think of straw. These **Cheese Straws** are great little nibbles and easy to make. Funnily enough, margarine works best in this recipe; butter is, well, too buttery and lard too lardy, so block margarine, is the one to use.

Grease a couple of baking trays and turn on your oven to 180-190C, 350-375F, gas 4-5.

Ingredients:

8 oz (225g) **self-raising** flour
¼ teaspoon salt
¼ teaspoon mustard powder
4 oz (113g) margarine, cut into small pieces
6 oz (170g) grated cheese (strong cheddar)
2 eggs, beaten

This is what you do:

Into a large bowl sift the flour, salt and mustard powder.

Add the margarine to the flour mixture, and rub it in until it resembles breadcrumbs, then add the grated cheese.

Add the beaten eggs.

Work everything together until you have a stiff pastry.

Flour your work surface and rolling pin and roll out the cheesy pastry quite thinly. You can cut shapes using pastry cutters (I used a Christmas Tree cutter) or finger-like strips.

Put them onto your greased baking trays and pop them in the oven for about 15 minutes.

And there you have it, or rather them, lovely cheese straws and biscuits.

19th December

Photograph by Rachel Mott

Luke 2:17-20
When they had seen him, they spread the word concerning what had been told them about this child, and all who heard it were amazed at what the shepherds said to them. But Mary treasured up all these things and pondered them in her heart. The shepherds returned, glorifying and praising God for all the things they had heard and seen, which were just as they had been told.

"Season's Greetings!" Mr Bungle beamed,
doffing his hat at the Christmas elf,
who stared disdainfully from the shelf,
offended at the cheek of it.
"Looks like snow," Mr Bungle said,
turning to talk to the fairy instead,
who scowled and tossed her gold-curled head,
too cross to agree the truth of it.
"I love Christmas, don't you?"
he asked of a robin clipped
to the tree, who
rather wisely
never said a word.

By Alison Mott

Festive Drinks

Heartwarmer:
This powerful punch serves about 12 people, depending on how big your glasses are:

Ingredients:
200 ml (about 7-8 fluid ounces) red grape juice
8 oz (225g) sugar
2 bottles of white wine (I like it to be quite dry)
1 bottle of red wine
350 ml (12 fluid ounces) dark rum

Put the grape juice and sugar into a large saucepan and heat until the sugar has dissolved. Add the rum.
Warm the wine in a separate saucepan (don't boil).
Mix the two together and serve hot.

Mulled Wine
A traditional drink at Christmas. There are numerous versions, but this is the one I prefer:

Ingredients:
2 bottles of red wine
½ glass of brandy
4oz (113g) sugar
3 sliced oranges
2 sliced Lemons
10 cloves
1 cinnamon stick
½ teaspoon ground ginger

Put everything into a large saucepan and heat, but do not boil.
Leave for a few minutes to let the spices infuse. Serve very warm. You can add hot water to 'lighten' it a little - if you really want to.

Goodnight Grog

Ingredients:
1½ pints of tea (strained if you are using leaf tea)
½ pint whisky (or dark rum is nice too)
2 tablespoons sugar (or you can use honey; the clear, runny kind)
1 cinnamon stick
1 teaspoon mixed spice (you can add more if you like it spicy)

Put everything into a saucepan and heat, but don't let it boil.
Remove from the heat and leave to let the cinnamon infuse.
Serve warm.

20th December

Photograph by Syd Spence

Matthew 2:1-2
The Magi visit the Messiah
After Jesus was born in Bethlehem in Judea, during the time of King Herod, Magi
from the east came to Jerusalem and asked, 'Where is the one who has been born
king of the Jews? We saw his star when it rose and have come to worship him.'

The wise men are usually seen as part of the nativity scene, although their visit is usually remembered at Epiphany (6th January).

The giving of gifts is another Christmas tradition and one form of gift is that of the traditional Christmas cracker.

Crackers were invented back in 1847 by Tom Smith, and not only for Christmas, but for other occasions too such as The Paris Exhibition in 1900, War Heroes in 1918 and The World Tour by Price Edward in 1926.

In 1830 Tom Smith worked in London as a boy in a bakers and confectioners and then started his own business as soon as he could. In 1840 he went to Paris and discovered sweets called bon bons, which were sugared almonds wrapped in tissue paper. He began to make and sell these in London and they did exceptionally well during the Christmas period.

Tom then put a message inside the paper; these were in the form of love mottos. One evening, when he threw a log onto his fire and it crackled, he came up with the idea of adding a 'spark' to the bon bons. Tom experimented tirelessly to find the right compound to 'pop' when the wrapper was broken open. This became the snap and the first cracker was created. He called them *Cosaques*. Tom decided not to include sweets anymore but to add a 'surprise' gift instead and keep the motto.

When Tom died he left the business to his three sons, Tom, Henry and Walter. Walter changed the love mottos to more topical ones. He also erected a drinking fountain in Finsbury Square in memory of his parents, Tom and Mary.

Raspberry, Chocolate and Vodka Mousse

Photograph by Kelly White

This recipe is not suitable for freezing, but can be made the day before.

Ingredients:

1 sachet gelatin (agar-agar can be used instead of gelatin if preferred.)
12 oz (340g) raspberries
1 oz (28g) cocoa powder
3 sachets hot chocolate powder
4 tablespoons sugar (you can use Canderel or Stevia for less calories)
500g pot natural fromage frais
1 tablespoon vodka (or gin if preferred)
1 egg white
2oz (56g) plain (dark) chocolate, grated.

Pregnant women, the elderly and babies are advised not to eat raw eggs, or consume vodka.

This is what you do:

Sprinkle the gelatin onto 4fl oz/113ml boiling water. Stir to dissolve and leave to cool.

Keep a few raspberries for garnish, lightly crush the rest and divide between 4 dessert glasses.

Sieve the cocoa and hot-chocolate powder into a bowl.

Add the sugar, fromage frais and vodka, and mix until smooth.

Add the cooled gelatin to the mixture and stir well. Whisk the egg white until stiff, and then fold carefully into the chocolate mixture with a metal spoon. Divide between the dessert glasses and chill for 2-3 hours until set.

To serve, garnish with the remaining raspberries and grated chocolate.

21st December

Matthew 2:3-6

When King Herod heard this he was disturbed, and all Jerusalem with him. When he had called together all the people's chief priests and teachers of the law, he asked them where the Messiah was to be born. 'In Bethlehem in Judea,' they replied, 'for this is what the prophet has written:
"'But you, Bethlehem, in the land of Judah,
are by no means least among the rulers of Judah;
for out of you will come a ruler
who will shepherd my people Israel."

Christmas, Natalis Domini

Christmas or *Christ's Mass* dates back to the 4th Century AD is one of the most popular Christian celebrations as well as one of the most globally recognised mid-winter celebrations. Christmas is the celebration of the birth of Jesus Christ, called the "Son of God," the second person of the Holy Trinity, as well as "Saviour of the World." The birth is observed on December 25, which was the Roman winter solstice when the Julian calendar was established.

Advent 21 is also the winter solstice in the northern hemisphere. It is the shortest day and the beginning of winter.

Boozy Coffee Cake

Grease and flour an 8-inch (20 cm) cake tin, spring-form is good, or one with a loose bottom.   Pre-heat the oven to 350F.

Ingredients:
For the cake:
4oz (113g) butter
4oz (113g) golden caster sugar
2 eggs, beaten
4oz (113g) self-raising flour

For the syrup:
150ml strong black coffee (Camp coffee works well)
4oz (113g) sugar (granulated is fine)
4 tablespoons whisky

For the cake:
Beat together the butter and sugar until the mix is light and fluffy.
Add the eggs and flour.
Put the mix into the greased tin and bake for around 20 minutes - until the cake springs back when pressed.
Leave it to cool on a wire rack.

To make the syrup:
Put the coffee and sugar into a small saucepan and bring to the boil. Keep stirring until all the sugar has dissolved. Boil for an extra minute then remove it from the heat and add the whisky.

Put the cooled cake onto a deep plate and pour over the coffee/whisky syrup. Leave it in a cool place to soak up the syrup - overnight is good.

Put the cake onto the dish you are going to serve it on, and serve with cream or ice cream.

22nd December

Photograph by Syd Spence

Matthew 2: 7-8

Then Herod called the Magi secretly and found out from them the exact time the star had appeared. He sent them to Bethlehem and said, 'Go and search carefully for the child. As soon as you find him, report to me, so that I too may go and worship him.' After they had heard the king, they went on their way, and the star they had seen when it rose went ahead of them until it stopped over the place where the child was.

Are we ready?

Are we ready,
for the day when it comes?
Have we done
all we can, to prepare?
We've shopped till we've dropped,
baked, wrapped and packed,
posted our greetings
to family and friends.
Baubles glowing, tinsel flowing,
lights twinkling in the night.
Everyone waiting.
Anticipating.
The joy of a gift – will it be all right?

Were they ready,
for the day when it came?
To be sent by a king, to find -
a child with lineage divine.
Balthasar from Arabia came;
Melchior's Persian perfume.
Gaspar brought oil from India's land,
they travelled from homelands so far.
Each one waiting.
Anticipating.
Knelt in homage – guided by a star.

Roasted Red Pepper and Tomato Soup

Set the oven to 180°C 350°F Gas 4

Ingredients:
2 or 3 Red Peppers
2 Ramiro Peppers
2lbs ripe tomatoes (about 1kg)
1 large onion chopped
1 or 2 carrots diced
2 rashers of lean un-smoked bacon - chopped
1 or 2 red chillies - depending on how 'hot' you like your soup – finely chopped
1 clove of garlic, crushed
2 tablespoons vegetable oil
1 pint of stock
Salt
Black pepper

To make the soup:

Cut the peppers in half and remove the stalks, core and seeds from the flesh. Put them onto a baking tray and roast in the oven for around 15 minutes – keep checking to make sure they don't burn and that they are done enough. Skin and de-seed the tomatoes by pouring boiling water over the them, leave for 5 minutes and then run cold water over the fruits. This will make them easy to peel and de-seed.

Top tip: you can used tinned, chopped tomatoes instead if you are short on time or cannot get fresh ones.

Pour the vegetable oil into a large saucepan and turn on the heat.
Add the onion, carrot, bacon and garlic and leave them to cook for a few minutes until softened.
When the peppers are roasted, peel off the skin and chop. Add the peppers, chopped chillies and tomatoes to the vegetable mix and stir
Add the stock and simmer for around twenty/twenty-five minutes.
Liquidise and add the black pepper.
If the soup is too thick, add a little milk.
Taste and add more seasoning if needed.

23rd December

Matthew 2:13-15
The Escape to Egypt

When they had gone, an angel of the Lord appeared to Joseph in a dream. 'Get up,'
he said, 'take the child and his mother and escape to Egypt. Stay there until I tell you,
for Herod is going to search for the child to kill him.'
So he got up, took the child and his mother during the night and left for Egypt, where
he stayed until the death of Herod. And so was fulfilled what the Lord had said
through the prophet: 'Out of Egypt I called my son.'

What's unusual about Rudolph?

A Yule log is a large and very hard log, which is burned as a part of traditional Christmas celebrations in several European cultures.

Prior to the 17th century there are no accounts of the custom in Great Britain and historians thought that the tradition was imported from Flanders in Belgium where it was very popular.

The first mention of the Yule log in Britain is a written account by the clergyman Robert Herrick, from the 1620s or 1630s. Herrick called the tradition a "Christmas log" and said that it was brought into the farmhouse by a group of males, who were then rewarded with free beer from the farmer's wife.

As the Yule log was thought to bring prosperity and protection to the family, then this would be so for a whole year if the remains of the log was kept for a year and then used to start the fire that would burn the new log.

There were also reports of competition between villagers to see who had the largest Yule log.

The expression *Yule log* has also come to refer to log-shaped Christmas cakes, also known as chocolate logs or Bûche de Noël.

And the unusual thing about Rudolph? He must have been a girl as only female deer with antlers are reindeer.

Bite-sized Chocolate Logs

Pre-heat the oven to gas 6, 400F/200C – that's a hot oven.
Grease Swiss-roll tin – that's a shallow tin, 13 inches x 9 inches (or 33 cm x 23 cm if you are metric). Line the bottom with greaseproof paper or baking parchment.

Ingredients:
6 medium, free-range eggs – separate the yolks from the whites. Whisk the whites in another bowl until they are firm stand up - and won't fall out if you tip it upside-down over your head.
6 oz (175g) caster sugar
6 tablespoons of cocoa powder – sifted
1 oz (25g) **plain** flour– sifted.
Half-a-pint (10 fl oz) double cream (300 ml) – whip it until stiff.

This is what you do:

In a large bowl whisk the egg **yolks** and caster sugar together really well until they are thick and creamy.
Add the sifted cocoa powder – it's best to sieve this again into your bowl to get more air into the mix. Gently fold the cocoa into the mixture.
Fold in the whisked egg whites followed by the sifted flour.
Pour the mixture into the Swiss roll tin and pop into the oven for 15 minutes.
When it's done (it will be well-risen and firm to the touch) remove from the oven and cover with a clean, damp tea towel and leave it to go cold.
Cut the sponge into six even rectangles (it's easiest to cut it down the middle lengthwise then across evenly twice).
Spread each strip with the cream and roll-up into logs, leaving the paper behind. If you would like a large log, which you can slice, just don't cut it up; spread it with cream and roll it up.

For the butter icing, you will need to put into a bowl:
6 oz (175 g) sifted icing sugar
8 oz (225 g) softened butter (room temperature is fine)
2 tablespoons sifted cocoa powder
Mix them all together and spread over the logs.
Dust them with icing sugar to give the snow-effect.

You can melt chocolate to pour over them instead if preferred.

24th December

This is a photograph I took of a brilliant painting by Artist **Soren Hawkes**.
To see more of his fabulous work (which you can buy) visit : http://passchendaeleprints.com

John 1: 1-5
In the beginning was the Word, and the Word was with God, and the Word was God. He was with God in the beginning. Through him all things were made; without him nothing was made that has been made. In him was life, and that life was the light of all mankind. The light shines in the darkness, and the darkness has not overcome it.

Ploegsteert Wood area, Flanders, Belgium, Christmas Eve, 1914 - a silence covered the land as shelling and rifle-fire ceased in some parts of the Western Front. Singing was heard from the enemy trenches; cigars and tobacco, buttons and badges were exchanged, when peace came down at Christmas.

Were they ready?

Were they ready
for the day when it came?
To pay the price -
the ultimate sacrifice.
In a land they didn't call home.
"It'll be over by Christmas,"
their loved ones believed,
but all of them knew:
their hopes were deceived.

Were they ready,
for the day when it came?
A quietness fell,
no sound of a shell.
Silence covered the land.
Then singing was heard
on the night of goodwill.
Exchanges made,
the night so still
When peace came down at Christmas.

Clever Salad

Christmas Eve is usually a time for a simple supper. I usually cook a ham or gammon joint, either roast it or, cook it in Cola in a slow cooker. This served with a cleverly presented salad is an excellent light evening meal.

To prepare the salad you will need:
Ramekin dishes – one for each person
1 whole cucumber
Enough grated carrot for each ramikin
Shredded lettuce
Sliced tomato
Thinly sliced radish.
If you like onion, thinly sliced red onion can be included.
Mustard cress.

Remove the peel from one side of the cucumber and slice it lenghtways so that you have a long strip for each ramekin dish. Line each dish with the cucumber.
Push some grated carrot into the bottom of each dish.
Add a layer of thinly sliced onion if you are using it.
Add enough shredded lettuce to fill the ramekin. Press it down well.
Turn out the ramekins onto each plate that you will be serving the ham or other delicacy (quiche is nice too, or a juicy steak). The carrot will be on the top and it will all be held together with the cucumber.
Put the thinly sliced radish onto the carrot, then the tomato and top with cress.
These individual salads will look impressive on your festive table.

25th December

John 1:14
The Word became flesh and made his dwelling among us. We have seen his glory, the glory of the one and only Son, who came from the Father, full of grace and truth.

It is thought that the first time Christmas was celebrated in Britain was in 521AD - in York.

The tradition of kissing under mistletoe is thought to be associated with Frigga, the Norse goddess of love, whose sacred plant it is.

Hanging up stockings on Christmas Eve comes from the Dutch custom of leaving shoes packed with food for St Nicholas's donkeys and he would then leave small gifts in return.

In the 12th-century French nuns also left socks full of fruit, nuts and tangerines at the houses of the poor.

5 x 5 x 5 x 5 Microwave Christmas Pud

For this quick and easy pud you will need a 1½ pint pudding basin, lightly greased. It also helps if you pop a circle of greaseproof paper into the base.

Ingredients:
3 oz (85g) **plain** flour
1½ oz (42g) fresh breadcrumbs – brown are best
½ teaspoon ground mixed spice
¼ teaspoon ground nutmeg
3 oz (85g) Demerara sugar
3 oz (85g) dark brown sugar (if you have it, if not use the sugar you have)
12 oz (340g) mixed fruit (raisins, sultanas, cherries, currants, etc. Chopped apricots are nice too)
1½ oz (42g) chopped nuts (optional)
1 small apple, peeled, cored and grated (or finely chopped)
Juice and grated rind of an orange
2 fl oz milk
3 oz (85g) butter (you can use margarine, but it won't taste as nice)
2 oz (56g) plain chocolate – yes, chocolate – chopped
1 medium egg, beaten.
2 tablespoons brandy or rum

This is what you do:
Sieve the flour and spices into a bowl and stir in the breadcrumbs, sugar, dried fruit, nuts apple and orange **rind**.

In a small microwaveable bowl, put the chocolate, butter, milk and orange juice. Microwave on 'de-frost' for 2½ minutes, until it's all melted.

Add the liquids to the dry ingredients and mix them all together. Add the beaten egg and brandy (or rum).

Spoon it all into your prepared basin and cover with greaseproof paper.

Microwave on full power for 5 minutes. Leave to stand for 5 minutes, then microwave for 5 more minutes.

Turn out and leave to stand for 5 minutes before serving with your favourite sauce.

26th December

Photograph by Syd Spence

Good King Wenceslas looked out, on the Feast of Stephen,
When the snow lay round about, deep and crisp and even.

Who was Good King Wenceslas and what is the Feast of Stephen?

Wenceslas died in the 10th century and was considered to be a matyr and a saint. He was, however only a Duke in his lifetime and the Holy Roman Emporor, Otto, gave him the royal dignity and title after his death. This is why he is called King Wenceslas in the song. A preacher from the 12th century told of his kind deeds and said that every night he 'rose from his noble bed' and, barefooted and with only one officer in attendance, he went round the churches and gave alms, money or food, to the poor; orphans, widows, prisoners and those who were ill or disabled. He was known as 'the father of all the wretched.'

Stephen is recognised as being the first Christian martyr. He was accused of blasphemy and at his trial he made a long speech denouncing those who were sitting in judgment on him. He was then stoned to death

St. Stephen's Day, or the Feast of St. Stephen, is a Christian saint's day to commemorate him and is celebrated on the 26th December, also known as Boxing Day.

Boxing Day was when servants and tradesmen received gifts known as a 'Christmas Box' from their employers. The term *Christmas-box*, dates back to the seventeenth century and it was a custom for tradespeople to collect 'Christmas boxes' of money on the first weekday after Christmas as a thank-you for their services throughout the year. Also, servants would have to wait on their 'masters' on Christmas Day so they were allowed to visit their families the day after and each servant would be given a box to take home, which contained gifts and often left-over food from Christmas Day.

St. Stephen's Day in Wales is known as *Gŵyl San Steffan*. An ancient Welsh custom, discontinued in the 19th century, included "holming" (the beating or slashing with holly branches) of late risers and female servants.

Turkey Curry

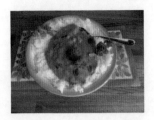

Ingredients:
Vegetable oil – 2 or 3 tablespoons to cover the base of the pan
3 large onions, chopped
2 cloves
2 cardamom pods
2 bay leaves
3 green chilies – finely chopped – you can take the seeds out if you prefer
1 clove of garlic – crushed
1-2 teaspoons of ground ginger
1-2 teaspoons Garam Masala
1 teaspoon turmeric
¼ teaspoon chili powder
Salt
1 tin of chopped tomatoes (more if you have lots of turkey)
Cooked, left-over turkey. (You can use un-cooked meat, chicken for example, but cooking will take slightly longer.)

For a vegetarian version, use cubed butternut squash and sweet potato

Here's what to do:
Heat the oil to a high temperature in a large, thick-based saucepan.
Add the chopped onions, cloves, cardamom and bay leaves and cook until golden.
Add the chopped chilies, garlic and ginger and cook until dark brown.
Make sure you keep stirring as the ginger will stick and burn if you are not careful.
Add the chopped tomatoes and Garam Masala, turmeric, salt and chili powder and stir together for about 5 minutes.
Add the turkey (or cubed veg) and cook for another 10 minutes, keep stirring.
Check your seasoning and add more chili if you like it hot, and maybe some salt, to suit your taste.
When you see the oil rising to the surface add a cup of **hot** water.
Stir then put the lid on and leave to simmer for 20-30 minutes (30-40 if you are using un-cooked meat, or even longer if you use lamb).
Stir occasionally during cooking.
Before serving, remove the cloves, bay leaves and cardamom pods.

Serve with rice – you can use fresh coriander for a garnish if you have any.
Also nice with a spoonful of yoghurt in the centre when you serve.

6th January

Epiphany

Photograph by Syd Spence

Matthew 2: 11-12
They went to the house where the child was and saw him with his mother, Mary. They bowed down and worshiped the child. They opened the gifts they brought for him. They gave him treasures of gold, frankincense, and myrrh. But God warned the wise men in a dream not to go back to Herod. So they went home to their own country by a different way.

There are many thoughts on how old Jesus was when this visit occurred. One thing we do know for sure is that it wasn't on the night of his birth and even though the Magi are usually depicted in any Nativity scene, he was probably between one and nine months old. Some even say two years.

Matthew's Gospel gives the only account of the Magi's visit and King Herod's wrath causing him to order that all male children under two be killed.

As Jesus was Jewish he would have been circumcised when he was eight days old, not necessarily in the temple, but at the house where they were staying. <u>House</u>, not stable - there lies another story. Mary and Joseph probably wanted to stay with relatives when they went to Bethlehem (David's town) to register, but as the town was so crowded, they would have had to sleep in the stable area, under the house.

Jesus would have been taken to the Temple thirty-three days later after the "days of purification" were completed, which is the 40th day after Jesus was born.

We don't know for sure how old Jesus was; Matthew's Gospel refers to him as a child, not baby, but we know the Magi followed a star, which at the time was not out of the ordinary to the untrained eye. Only they, who studied the stars, would have noticed it and recognised it as having special relevance.

Galette des Rois

Photograph: Creative Commons

The French serve Epiphany Cake on the 6th January, Twelfth Night, called *Galette des Rois* (Cake of Kings)

It can be quite a complicated recipe, but here's a simpler version.

You will need:

1lb 2oz/500g puff pastry (or flaky pastry) - either shop-bought or home made
3 oz/75g caster sugar
2 oz/50g soft, unsalted (if poss) butter
4 oz/100g ground almonds
1 egg

Here's what to do:
Preheat the oven to 210C/410F/Gas 7
Divide the pastry in two parts; roll each out into a circle about 9in/23cm across and put one circle on to a baking tray.
Beat the egg and remove a small amount for glazing. Mix in the almonds, sugar and butter until you have a smooth paste. Spread the paste over the pastry on the baking sheet leaving about half-an-inch round the edge uncovered. Pop a bean, or coin, or small figure into the paste, wet the edge and lay the second circle on top. You can make a pattern on the top or just leave it plain. Glaze with the remaining egg yolk and pop into the oven for about 30 minutes until crisp and golden.

Serve warm with cream or ice-cream.

Whoever finds the bean or coin in their slice will be king or queen for the night.

Karen Ette worked in catering before taking a Higher National Diploma in Business Studies. She then worked in Educational administration before returning to Loughborough University to undertake her MA in Creative Writing. She went on to complete her PhD, also at Loughborough and has written a novel, short stories, magazine articles and university guides. She is a member of the Leicester Writers' Club and Western Front Association.

She lives in the Midlands and runs creative writing workshops as well as speaking on Leicestershire in the First World War.

Thank you for buying The Advent Calendar Recipe Book. If you have enjoyed it, it would be appreciated if you would please take a moment to review it. Thank you.

LONDON IN VERSE